Love's Twisted Lessons:
(For the Heartbroken, the Heartbreaker's, and the Sexually Frustrated)

By Danielle Cooper

ISBN: 978-0-578-09769-5

Cover design by Danielle Cooper

Dedicated to:
The heartbroken, because love
can make you crazy, even split personality
crazy. And people often forget that heart
tipped arrows aimed at the heart, even
from cupid, are still arrows aimed at the
heart...

Table of Contents:

Welcome to *Love's Twisted Lessons: For the Heartbroken, the Heartbreaker's, and the Sexually Frustrated.* First and foremost I would like to Thank You for supporting the book, it really means a lot.

....

I would also like to extend my sincerest apologies if your reasons for picking up this book include: getting your heartbroken or being sexual frustrated. I understand that these are very troubling and difficult times that you're going through right now (or have experienced). Equally important, if you have discovered that all the pain, heartache, and frustration your going through is somehow apart of your karma, I would like to applaud you on the realization however still extend my sympathies as you go through your storm of Karmatic payback.

If you're reading this book and <u>HAVE NOT</u> been in love, I have to be honest when I say that it can go to the places explored in this work, and beyond; but it's a hell of a ride and can be a life altering experience (For the better or the worse, depends on if you learned the lesson

for you). And last but certainly not least, Thank you for those who found comfort, voice, guidance or just good ol' fashion fun through my work. I strongly encourage that you read with a pen and write all over the pages, fill in the blanks, jot down stuff, draw, or anything that will help your healing process or casual reading.

Lastly, for the heartbreakers, if you get caught, you're SO on your own, so cover your tracks or at the very least get your lies down.

Good luck on your journey, Happy hunting, and Happy Reading!

-Danielle Cooper

Fine Print: I **am not** being held responsible or liable for the actions of others if you give ANY of the works from this book to a partner, significant other, or fuck buddy to express how you feel.

ALSO, if you receive a cute poem that speaks of forever, marriage, ryde or die, etc. only for the

person to use you for sex, money, or whatever; that shit isn't my fault either.

HEARTBROKEN

Random Thoughts of a Heartbroken Mind:

You ever been rocked by your sadness into a nightmare of love's despair? Only to awaken to a reality that isn't far off from the dreamscape you left? Heartbroken and miserable, I'm there.

No one is ever ready for love…. NO ONE. No one is prepared for the shutters that come along your sides when they touch. No one is prepared for the tunnel vision. NO ONE. Not the wisest man or the scholar. Because love… Turns people into fools because it doesn't involve the mind, it's all heart. It's feelings and emotions in their purest and devilish of forms.

At the end when (and if) you've survived love's storms. There is no guarantee that your heart will be intact. No guarantee that you will still be left standing or able to live another day. So be careful and choose wisely.

Your Thoughts:

_____
_____
_____
_____
_____
_____
_____
_____
_____
_____
_____
_____
_____
_____
_____
_____
_____
_____
_____
_____

BANG!!! BANG!!!! BANG!!!!!!
(Punching holes in sheet rock wall)
BANG!!! SPLAT!!!!!
(Phone hits the wall, then the floor)

IF you don't call me back. Send me a fucking text message, a smoke signal or something. I.... I.... I... will go insane. Think I already have, which is why I can't handle this bullshit anymore. I....I.....I..... Just need to hear your voice. See you. Have you near. But...You refuse to give me the little I need to go about my day and function properly, function normally. Instead you leave me like this. A version of myself I never knew existed while trapped playing this game. It's gotten so bad that my church, family, and friends have started to question my levels of self-esteem, my mental stability. And I've... IGNORED their warnings of how you will ultimately be my downfall. Of how I have turned into a crazed zombie, only wanting and searching for you. FUCK THEM. And YES!! I know; that this ignorant bliss of mine will ultimately cause them to call the hospital; for me, for a visit from the nice men in the white coats, who will carry me away kicking and screaming for 48-72 hour observation, or maybe an extended stay. But I don't care, because YOU are the only cure for this broken heart, bruised ego, and loss of pride. I CARE ABOUT YOU. This above all, is why I just can't handle your ability to be so fucking cold. I would appreciate, if you at the LEAST showed me some fucking respect! Just reach back to my outstretched hand, please?

=(...=O...>=(

O really?!?! YOU CAN'T DO THAT!?!?!?!? Do you really believe your ex or those other hoes hold a fucking candle to me?! I will murder them in the street! I have decided; you will no longer be acquainted with my calm demeanor. I.....I.....I..... Will get you, you will be mine.

However until then, I am lost. Stuck in this with no clear direction out and I don't know who I am anymore. I couldn't close my eyes without seeing your face, so now I don't sleep. Can't go anywhere without seeing you, being reminded of you. So; I...I...I....am running away, to destinations unknown. With my phone (in the event that you might call) and my IPOD that blasts a sad love song heartbreak playlist that will surely bring me to tears.

Goodbye to the city lights we once enjoyed
together, I've ventured to nature's wooded oasis with tear
streaming to SCREAM!!!!!!!
AAAAAAAAAAAAAAAAHHHHHHHHHHHHHHHHHHH
HHHHHH!!!!!!!!!!!!!! WHY THE FUCK WON'T SHE
CALL ME!!!!!!!!?!????! WHAT DID I DO WRONG!?!?!?
WHY CAN'T SHE RECOGNIZE THAT I AM GOOD
FOR HER?!?!!?!!??
My cries are interrupted by friends hounding me, who I
originally thought would console me, bring comfort and
understanding. Only to discover they don't have a fucking
kind word to say. "Fuck that bitch" Is NOT what I need to
hear. Their phone calls and texts go unanswered. Cause,
they, don't need to see or hear me like this. They wouldn't
understand anyway. You....You.....You... are the only one I
want to hear from. You... are the only one I want near.
You... are my medicine. And without you, I can't move.
I question my worth now more than ever in this stagnant
state. Because I can't figure out what's wrong with me?
Why can't you love me like I want you too? I mean, I
don't want to be with anyone else but you. So why don't
you feel the same?
chuckle It's funny, deep down I know that... As I wait
by my phone your fingers are dialing someone else's
number; as I wait for your text; Your laughing your ass off
texting her; and as I cry at the fact that I have lost myself
in this love for you, in this want for you, in this desire for
you. You have already moved on.
Despite all the energy I put forth, trying to
form us, holding onto our memories training my brain
never to forget our moments. I am not on your mind at all.
This makes my heart stretch me past the point of dilution. I
didn't think I could compromise all of me..... Especially for
love that won't be returned. Forcing awkward reunions
upon us so that I might prove myself worth to you, but you
don't even think I'm worth a phone call, after peak hours,
when your minutes are free. Love, once again promised me
a love to call my very own. I just should have specified

that she was supposed to feel the same.
Damn.

~If you haven't ever felt like this, haven't ever wanted
someone who isn't ready to be with you, isn't feeling you.
If you can't relate to a Choux Pastry Heart, being Crushed
Out, having Unanswered Questions, had someone MAKE
A FOOL OF YOU, been BITTER. THAN FUCK
YOU!!!!!!!!!
I hope Love SLAPS THE SHIT OUTTA YOU.
Because you won't understand this,
CAN'T understand it.
TIL IT HAPPENS TO YOU.

I Found my Goddess

I
Found her
While searching through cyberspace
Finding love in all the wrong places
And
She, appeared
One of the few women
Not using her ass
As bait
To catch friend requests
Her truth and contradictions scattered across her page
She was
Open.
And then I read her poem
And was sold
Gave her my number
Cause the whole
Back and forth
Via email
Was getting old
I had to
Hear her voice
And it swam around
Knocking to and from
In my mind
It made me imagine
What she felt like
Looked like
While holding hands
Down crowded city streets
In her poem
Screamed God-like perfection
In all that human pain
Her voice…
Allowed me to bathe in the sounds of a Goddess
And sent me back to childhood school days
When shit was a little simpler
And friends were lost and made again in the same day

Healed with cookies, candy, ice cream, and cakes
Or a simply heavy contract of
I'm sorry
And
I forgive you
It brought me back to a time when
My invincibility was not a question
It was a fact
When I was bolder
When fears of rejection,
Broken hearts, and disappointments
Didn't exist
But she also...
Kept me present
Wanting to stay in the moment
To be serenaded with words
Driven by her
Pen-cil.
Then I HAD to see
Her
In order to pay homage to the human form
That traps her divinity
I wanted her spirit to dive into
Me
Meet with mine
And
Intertwine
Binding us to a contract
My spirit
Scribbled on ripped pages
The last time we met a goddess
It states:
We are one.
Reconnected
Reincarnated
Lovers

Please don't leave me again.
(sign at the bottom)
But she didn't sign it.
And as long as I had her
I didn't mind it

The Little I Know

The little I know
Is that I am not human
This body
Fake
An illusion in the minds of the creatures I surround myself with
I know this
Because
It reacts differently
To pain
I know.
A woman's beauty is in her scars
So to church I go
To watch their tears flow as pain and trauma overwhelms them
To points where outcries might reach the heavens unknown,
As motherless women mourn the loss of themselves
I know that
This,
Is more captivating,
Arousing,
Beautiful, then any view on this planet
The little I know is....
Words are more powerful than fists
And I long for a physical pain that
Would ever
Match my emotional
because words have cut a hole in my psyche
That caused me to further be unable to feel,
Unable to grieve
unable to love.
But always able to write
The little I know is....
Emotional pain is my muse

My secret weapon
allowing my words to evolve
Into something more
Then I usually permit

Allowing me to rip across skin to the white meat
Scrawling words across paper
With pieces of my heart and mangled flesh dribbling off
The page
Unable to catch it all
The Little I know is....
That on sunny days I saw love....
Through broken glass, screams and tears
Through busted eyes, black lips
They beat me cause they loved me
They beat each other caused they loved each other
But What I know for sure is that.....
With you...
I don't like pain as much
With you...
I'd rather not see tears flow
With you...
I do not need pain nor misery to write
With you...
The most beautiful view is being trapped in your gaze
With you....
I finally feel a part of this planet
I feel like a woman
I feel human
But only with you...
And this,
Is all I know,
and all I care to know.

IF

IF
My hair was longer
Stomach flatter
Thighs thinner
Body toned
Would that keep your eyes from wandering?
Diction better
Tongue faster
Vocab. more developed
Would that make you want to talk to me?
IF
I was more musically inclined
Artistically gifted
Would you fight to be my inspiration?
While your eyes wander, hands caress,
My heart feels..
You touching, holding, kissing, laying with another
So
Between tear soaked playlists,
Dampened spirits,
And
Tweet cigarette breaks destroying this body
I find myself asking...
IF
I could cook better
IF
I could dance better
Move, rock, and shake my assets like that of my ancestors
Would you move to my beat?

IF
I was flexible,
Would you show me the same love I show you?
Bend to MY desires?
IF
My legs stretched back into pretzel like forms,

Reflecting my willingness to compromise beyond my limits
Splitting me in two
Would that interest you?
If... If... If...
I loved myself
It wouldn't be so hard for me to admit
That..
It wouldn't matter
IF
I did half those things.
Your eyes would still wander.
Hands still touch, caress, and hold
Another
But soon.
Your touch will grow cold to me.
And I will be forced by my self-respect to leave
But not until
I fully accept that
I cannot be comforted by eyes and hands that wander
But I can't leave before then
Not until this turns to ashes
Burnt to nothingness by your blind passion
And while I wait
I grow weary and restless
Turning sour then angry
Ready to break, fight, scratch, and kill
Enraged and bitter about a love that left and did not return.
Because despite my have not's I had so much more.
So much more...

That I was willing and able to give you.

In (a)_____

In (a)_____ you made me forget about her
Causing tears to be no more
I allowed myself to melt in your arms
Hesitant to believe your words at first
Only to believe them at ungodly hours
As we spoke
Sharing secrets and scars
I believed you when you called me beautiful
In (a)_____ I was able to write
Without pains presence
Able to smile at the end of a sad poem
In (a)_____
I didn't mind that my truth wasn't pretty
In (a)_____
I started planning trips with you
Wanting to escape, explore, discover with you
In (a)_____
However
Feelings
Got involved
Shattering our sterile bubble of comfort and ecstasy
I see now, that you knew
That it's easy to share bed and secrets
With someone you don't plan on being with
So
Like a tampon
You thought I was disposable
Bled your words on to me
Allowed me access to your most intimates
Stained me with your truth
Then, feeling I was becoming too familiar
You couldn't handle the disease of feelings
This sent you into a panic
So before you went into shock with love
You ripped me out
And threw me away.

Rant... My Worth

Your silence was marked by the loss of your voice and phone today. Maybe now I can tolerate not hearing from you. But I can't. I can't help feeling like this was a strange sign of conversations never to come. Of a response that I am not ready for nor want to hear. I know I'm not ready to hit your wall. Didn't know it would come so soon. A_____ ago it was rainbows and butterflies and now, nothing. Not even reminisce of what used to be. Our recent interactions have been an empty shell of what they once were. So now I'm fighting the urge to come see you. Fighting the urge to call you, and use the money (that I made specifically so I could see you), to see you. But I just don't believe that you want to see me and that hurts. I believe that you no longer need my touch at night. No longer need nor want to be in my arms. But you told me I held you the best. I guess you are more comfortable protecting yourself in the arms of another. I have unanswered questions that plague my mind causing spasms of doubt and awkwardness. I didn't want it to be like this, didn't want to end on these terms. Shit I'm still unclear if we are ending, or did end at all. But apparently I'm confused as to when we actually began in the first place. So... :/ But these unanswered questions are really causing me to question, me. Am I worth a phone call, a text, even a stupid message on facebook from you? Am I worth a trip to _____? Am I worth the letting down of your walls? Am I worth anything? I ask these questions to myself, knowing that my mouth will never speak such words of frustration to your face. Out of fear you will take offense and never talk to me again, even though you barely talk to me now. But really, am I not worth a chance? *Obviously not,* because your spending time elsewhere, with "safer candidates". This news has devastated me to a point stuck somewhere between shock and numbness. I really wanted my body to know your touch, I loved seeing you when I woke up in the morning. I felt safe in your arms. I thought I was worth more to you than this. More than this distance, as I stand here stupidly with hopes of

unity; hopes that the days of searching for love are over. I thought, I found something unique, something special. I thought you felt the same. Yet even though I know this, I still have these unanswered

questions that keep me trying to come back to you. They make me
want to prove you wrong.
My worth.....
If measured by the way other people treat me
I am worth
A smile
Because it only takes 26 muscles to do so
A call back
After a night of pleasure
Since that only requires a push of a button
A text (without smiley faces)
To make sure I got somewhere
Safe
A hug (a Christian one)
To show affection without showing me love
Dinner
To be energized
For a night spent working it off
Long walks
Only to get to the destination of your bed
I'm worth...
Nothing really
Not anything that matters
I'm not worth the truth
Everyone hidden behind walls and false images
I've never really seen anyone
I'm not worth commitment
Cause no one is faithful, not even me
I'm not worth meeting your parents

Cause I'm too _____ for their taste
I'm not worth
The safety of your arms
Because THEY feel,
Which makes YOU feel
I am not worthy
I am not WORTH the risk
Because..... I don't know why
I'm not worth love because

Fuck I don't know
Nor do I care at this point. My real worth; is every fucking tear cried, its every fucking chance given and then some. I am worth the visions of rainbows, butterflies, and transformation. Long walks to views that I LOVE. I'm worth something I'm not exactly sure what yet. But I know it's more than the bullshit people try to give me. I know damn well, I, am worth more than your bullshit excuses about your inability to feel. I am worth the truth about your intentions. I am worth getting back the effort that I put in. I am worth my time given. I am worth every fucking orgasm given. I am worth your heart, mind and soul. You really didn't want to know how much I was worth because you knew you couldn't afford me. So without knowing my true value, I declared you my love and gave you a layaway option on my
forever. Assuming you would pay the balance in full sooner or later.
Chuckle
Shame on me.

Random Thoughts of a Heartbroken Mind:

I ate 387 Hersey's kisses for all the times you introduced me as
your misses. 254 Oreos for the times you said you wouldn't leave me for
other bitches. Explored the depths of our relationship at the bottom of
an ice
cream carton and I'm still not full.
Feasted on the fruits of lovers trying to find the sustenance you once
provided between their legs and I'm still not full.

My eyes have seen love in action; I've seen its tricks, its games. I
have been played by it. With scars still visible, these eyes have
grown wise to the sorrow that love brings and are tricked no more.
But this heart... This heart, even in pieces follows love blindly.
Through the storms and hurricanes it will gladly follow. And while
it endures, I lose pieces of me, along the way, never to be seen
again.

While agonizing over sappy love movies, I wait to exhale. With
meshell inspired playlists of pain that turn any day into a rainy
afternoon as your absence makes my heart grew fonder.

Your Thoughts:

_____
_____
_____
_____
_____
_____
_____
_____
_____
_____
_____
_____
_____
_____
_____
_____
_____

How Do You Leave a Goddess?

How do you leave a goddess?
When she is your inspiration
The air you breathe
Your shooting star
Allowing all your wishes to come true
How do you leave a goddess?
When the words I love you
mean nothing
They are empty
Replaced by
I see you.
And you see her
Even when she's not there
Her smell in the air
Your senses working off
The memory of her
How do you leave a goddess?
Who doesn't see the god in you
But is connected
Knowing the reasoning behind all the shit you do
Because she knows your depth
And has taken the time to hear the stories that run through you
How the fuck do you leave her?
The Divine
The one who takes up the left and right side of your mind
That makes your heart stutter
Almost stopping
As she glides by
How do you leave a goddess?
The answer is.
You don't, you can't
Despite the flesh you will feed on
To get over her
To feel again
No one will match her

While desperately trying

To find a connection with another
All you will think about is her.
How you wish your head
Was between her legs
Tasting her waters
There will be no peace
As you attempt to kill parts of your humanity
in order to become more godlike
So that your universe
can return
AND
These near fatal attempts
Will be met
With anger and frustration
Because she never wanted to be your goddess
You are just a human to her
And despite the light
That she see's inside of you
She is waiting for you to see it in yourself.
But you can't cause
Your heart and mind
Are finally in agreement on one thing
And that is
No sunrise looks as beautiful
Unless she is there to enjoy it with you
To wake up in the morning
Is not as much of a blessing
Unless
She is there beside you
And lastly
No one will know you
See you
As clearly
As she does
So how the fuck do you leave a goddess alone
Who has found another
To worship?
As you
Deal with human inadequacy

Mind fucking yourself
Stupid

With questions of why?
What is it about that girl/guy?
That makes your goddess
Long to be by their side
Instead of yours.
The truth of the matter is
You can't, leave because
Your heart is still there
So
Time will heal the wound
Of you expecting to share a lifetime with her
Only to find out
Your paths have crossed only once
And you
cannot leave your path
To jump onto hers
Chasing her into
Eternity
Changing the course of her future
While destroying your own
Really, all you can really do
Is change your religion
To one of self
Find the god/goddess
In you
Speak positivity into your existence
and hope
and pray
that, that's enough
And allow time
To do its thing.

Say Something... Song Thang

Say that I'm broke
Say my sex is a joke
Just say something
To release me.

For 5 long weeks
I have been wondering
"WHY THE FUCK DONT YOU CALL ME ANYMORE!!!???!"
Bitch your dragging my heart on Dante's floor
I don't want to do shit anymore
Unless it's with you
Just say something
Nigga your breath stink
Something
To let me know what to do

Say that I'm broke
Say my sex is a joke
Just say something
To release me

Baby why you playin me
I thought that we were meant to be
When I look up to the stars
It's your name I see
So please
Let me know
Why
You iggin me?

Say that I'm broke
Say my sex is a joke
Just say something
To release me

The homies like you
(So, why you iggin me?)

My family would dig you
(So, why you iggin me?)
I like vegetarian too!
(So, why you iggin me?)

Say...
Say something
To release me from this pain
So when the homies ask
Why they don't see you anymore
I can explain
I can say....
She said the sex was tight
But she wasn't dealing with my craziness
So she had to take flight
She was cool with textin all night
But when I commented on almost all her facebook pics
That set off a red light
When I was late to almost every date we had
She blew her whistle and threw her flag
And when I added my feelings at the tip
She said fuck this
Saw another artsy chick
And abandoned ship
Damn.

Another Sad Like Poem

I...
Thought of you today...
Your smile.
Sent me to bitter sweet memories
Of when
I
Made you smile
Causing my heart to flutter
I liked the way you laughed
It was cute..
It always made me smile
I liked the way you smelled
My nostrils sending signals to my crotch
After just one sniff.
Now
I pass many that wear your scent
But they don't smell as good as you
I miss your
Eyes.
They
Pulled me in
A couple times during sex
I thought our souls connected
You stared a hole through me
Allowing me to be fully present
Burning a hole in my memory
I can't forget them
Especially now since

You won't even look at me
I tried to catch your gaze once
But...
Your eyes averted mine
Causing my heart to drop
As I understood
I had been replaced
Now

Someone **else's** eyes
Are being passionately stared into
By you.
Someone **else** knows
The warmth of your touch
Someone **else** is seeing you
Smile
Making you smile
Sigh
I miss talking to you
Your vocab.
Sick
Mind fucking me every time we spoke
Your poetry
Sent shivers up my spine
As you…
Commanded the stage
Throwing your voice
I wanted to say
THAT's My Baby!!!!!
Tapping my neighbor to brag
"Aint She something!!!!"
But you…
Sadly aren't, Mine.
A fact that.
Produces a lump in my throat
That isn't easily swallowed away
But the tears refuse to come
Because I liked you
Didn't love you
But the pain of
Being dropped
By such a bad bitch
With the super geeky swag
Hurts me
And
My ego
Sending a pulsating ache through my chest
And that hurt, feels all the same

Momma Watched

I died a while back
Long before the actual
Physical emergency room visit
My mother watched this
With stone cold eyes
Piercing my soul
She could do nothing but watch
And verbalize the shame that
I found out later was her secret silent pain
She
Did all she could to warn me
About man
His harsh realities
Trapping her in a constant maternal position
Taking care of him and his babies
Giving up friends and family
To keep and start his
I learned her lessons well
But she
Didn't expect this....
ME
Loving women
Getting trapped in their
Sweet misery
Leaving
Only to return more broken than I was before
Leaving parts of me she loved and nurtured at an ex's door
Or pieces of me scattered on their bedroom floor
And she saw this
And now I understand why she hated my euphoric moments of
bliss
Because she foresaw that it would end like this
Me holding on for dear life on the end of a kiss
I now understand no sane mother could watch this

And not miss
The daughter that once was

The strong woman that used to be
Before love had me strung out
Showing my gratitude stuck on my knees
Begging for her forgiveness while attempting to keep their
allegiance
My words to her now
Mean nothing
Credibility torn to shreds
After the many times I stood at her doorstep
Swearing I was clean
From loves poisons
Momma watched
and had hope
That everything was fine
Things were going okay
Until I received a call from love
Packed my shit
And some of hers'
and ran away.
I am such a fiend for loves pain
Now when I do speak to her
She rarely says my name
With the dull pain and understanding that the little girl
She named_____ would never be the same
In her words sometimes
I hear her asking different questions
But can't do so amidst all the bottled up rage
Pain, Anger, Disappointment, Resentment
Because I was supposed to be the strong one
The smart one
The gifted one
The talented one
The one to erase her past mistakes
Make it so she didn't sacrifice all
For nothing
I was the one she was grooming this world for
And now.
She has to change the locks on the door
Due to fears that I might come back for more

Understanding addiction all too well
Her family cycle continues
She only wishes that my score came from the needle
Instead of a lover's eyes
At least it would be easier to let me go
Easier to forget the daughter behind
As I continue to get lost and high in this
Emotional, mental, and physical slow suicide

Just A FUCK?!?!

Just a fuck
What the fuck
You mean you was slobbin on my pussy
For hopes of good luck
Your telling me
You didn't like my mind
I was just a nut.
What the fuck
What you mean I was just a fuck?
You couldn't tell me that
So I
Could prepare myself before feelings attacked
Didn't think info
Of you having fucked up
Ulterior motives
Would come back
Couldn't have told me this
In the beginning
Had me thinking a was winning
A prize
One of those
Will open the door from the other side
Bronx Tale
Great one's by my side
Damn
Your actions sure did tell a big fat lie
Of decades of us sleeping side by side
Sigh
I wish
You would've told me
Shouldn't have found out through
Mutual friends
Trying to help
But
Seeming noisy

But they had to tell me the truth
And for me to find out that I was the other, other woman
Made me want to punch a wall and pull out a tooth
All you had to do was tell me the truth
And for a while there
After I knew
I just wanted to smell your air
Be your friend
Exchange stories
Of past lovers and current crushes
Over,
high-priced Thai food
I just wanted to hang
But you have made it impossible for me to say your name
Without feeling hella disrespect and some type of pain
I don't know what happened to you
Who raped your innocence causing you to be this cold
I don't know what happened to you
Which Goddess broke your heart
Causing you not to feel anymore
To stomp hearts
While they're at your feet
Begging for your love
I don't know whose secret you were
Causing you to feel less than
Who beat you?
And with every punch and kick
Bled your humanity out a little bit
I was just a fuck
But the fact that I was
Despite what your actions showed
Makes me wanna ask
Who hurt you?
Causing the pain
That you now cause
Laced with
This constant hunger
What did they do?
Because the cool person I met...

There is just certain shit that they wouldn't put people through
But
I only saw what you wanted me to see
But I thought I saw through that
Falling for, not the person that you are now
But the one you're on your way to be
Which is why me being just a fuck
Hurts but
Doesn't faze me
Cause the person I saw
Has yet to be
But I was just a fuck
So the person I am waiting for
I doubt I will ever meet.

You Were Right/ Should Have….

I should have listened to your words instead of.
Getting distracted by that sweet voice
Mesmerized by the way your mouth moved
And getting lost in your eyes.
Should have figured you were too honest
I didn't read your actions and responses correctly.
Because I was blinded by your beauty when the sun hit your brown skin
Should have seen the revolving door, chaos in your eyes
But you looked so peaceful in your sleep
Should have listened
Your poems,
They foreshadowed what was to come
But the poem you wrote to me.
Made my heart drop
Gave me Goosebumps
And made me want to be near you
So I could hear more
I should have listened
Fooled by your big butt and smile
I didn't see this happening
My emotions leading to
Ignored phone calls and unanswered messages
You creating distance
Igging me
You attempting not to feel
Not to live
Not to allow yourself to slip, trip, and fall
Burying your emotions for me into the bodies of others
Causing my psyche to lose itself
Trying to understand what happened
To the us

I thought we were trying to form
I wanna ask..
How many people have been in your bed after me?
Hearing your screams and moans of ecstasy?

How many have you written poems too?
Sent sad smiley face messages to say "I miss you"?
How many have gazed into your eyes
And been broken in your presence?
As you speak about the beauty of life
Yet never experience it
Never letting go
Never truly feeling
So afraid of feeling pain that you cause it.
Turning good girls bad
Now they're gone forever
Because past hurts haunt you, causing
Ghosts to appear every time you smile
Being reminded of times when you were happy with her
Only wanting **her** and the remnants of Yall relationship
Abandoning this when you realize
I, We are not her.
I....
Am sorry for the pain you felt, that she caused
That led to the unstoppable flow of tears
Numbness
The guard dogs, walls, snipers, electric fences, land mines around
your heart
And this bitter ass game you play
Breaking hearts that come around her way
Telling us to go when your words and actions told us to stay
I...
Should have read between the lines
Should have saw the truth, behind the bitterness in your eyes
You; don't want to feel
So,
I guess
You were right...
Hearts do get broken around you

But that's only because as you walk
Everyone is concentrating on your ass
So no one noticed the big ass hammer in your hand
I was too hooked on your smile

I let my guard down for awhile
Allowing my heavy heart to rest on my sleeve
And then...
SPLAT!!!......
And no one..
Including me..
Was prepared for that.

-By the Founding member of_____ broke
my heart, support group, foundation, non-profit, and substance
abuse group

Did It Really Not Happen/I Remember..

Did it really not happen?
People tell me it didn't
But I don't believe them
Because I remember
That it was you
Who made me stare for a second too long
You can't possibly be the person they say you are
However, when I bring up conversations
And things I remember hearing you say
You have no recollection
Then I start to think this didn't happen
But I remember
Us battling through fits of inadequacy
Parental pressures and loneliness
Did those things not really happen?
I mean people say.
I never met you
But I thought I saw you
I mean really saw
You
Lost time with you
Days seeming like hours
No one can explain to me
Why I remember your
Testimonies of hardship and perseverance
Or the scar on your belly
I still don't understand how this didn't happen
Cause your eyes, still hold this picture
Of paradise, happiness, peace, forever
......
I just no longer see you in my dreams
Burying our memories
With the understanding that there will be
No present, no future
Only this reality

Where I no longer see you

In the faces passing by
Forced to forget
Given no choice
Sick of
Everyone seeing me as crazy
Because I remember
That this did happen
That I have your secrets never shared
And this
A, lone picture of our bliss
Unhealthy I know
A little crazy I know
But
It shows you
Looking at me
With eyes struck by happiness and awe
Taken prior to the truth that I have now
While in our honeymoon phase
You
Gave me a look
That can only be described as
A love looking at their lover
It showed our connection
Even though brief
And I am comforted by this
Because despite all the memories of you
That I must forget
To function
To love again
To move about this world
I have this
Moment
Captured in time
When our love was present and visible
So fuck what they say about you
The evils they tell
Because in all that
I have this...
A moment when the beast they describe

Had a softness in her eyes
That looked real enough
To be something more

<u>Untitled</u>

I remember when I was held by those arms.
kissed by those lips
and made hole by her presence
such a long time has passed since I've been held
and felt safe in someone's arms.
It's hard sometimes to look at her picture
to see the beauty
That caused so much pain
It's still something my mind cannot comprehend as of yet
But somehow I still love her
and have found a way to miss her
her voice, her energy, her aura, her everything
I still remember when I was hurt by that face
chocked by those hands
lied to by those lips
and ripped apart by her truth
I still remember when my love turned to hate
Yet I can still tell you how she influenced me,
And why
and how I will never be the same because of her
I do hate her
But
Still need her near,
want to be held but also want to harm
and this is the nature of my relationship with her
for she was the only one given my heart, body, and soul
But she bruised my body and
ripped out a piece of my soul
and
Broke my heart
She is the only one
I let
Truly know me

We Can't Be Friends

We can't be friends.....
We can't be friends because
I still remember how your kisses felt
Soft, smooth, and juicy
I still remember how you used to hold me
Tight with strong arms that gave me the illusion of safety
I still remember how you look, coming out the shower after a long
day
Dripping wet, with your favorite towel draped around your waste
We can't be friends because truth,
Be told
I still have scars from
The internal emotional hemorrhaging
You caused
WE can't be friends because
I can't handle
Seeing you happy
It may cause PTSD flashbacks of our misery
Which will motivate me sabotaging your bliss
We can't be friends because I
Remember the pain I felt when we had to part
A pain greater than the agony experienced when together
WE can't be friends because it _____ to get over you
We can't be friends because it would once again be an unhealthy
situation for me
And finally,
We can't be friends
Because I have learned to love myself more than you.

(JK, I still want to be your friend) ☺

I Need to Tell You

I need to tell you
I need to tell you
I need you
More than the air I
Breathe
I Love You
Yes I said it
I fucking LOVE YOU
And remember I said it
Because after this I won't let
You forget it
I Love You
So much
I will share You
Open relationships
No titles
Don't mean Shit
I don't care Boo
Cause I know my shit is great
And I will learn tricks and splits
To keep you
I can handle
Your dates and stupid admirers cause
I...
Will keep you
Coming back home
Just be real with me
On those nights when you leave me alone
That you are with another chick

Making her
Shrink to her knees and moan
And I'll stand tall
Proud in it all
That I went through all this
For those moments of heaven tainted bliss
When I look into your eyes and melt

Cause you let me bring out a different side of myself
After mind fucking intermissions
Of peaceful healing revelations
I need...
Your kisses
For everything to be alright
They will comfort me
Through the lonely nights
Where our physical distance
Isolates us to memories
And
hands confined to
Body alone
I just needed to tell you
This
So I could
Finally..
Breathe

Facebook Stalker

I am your facebook stalker
AND NO PISS ASS firewall blocker can keep me from you
I have three different pages
To keep track of you
Bitch I made sure we had mutual friends
Who help out a great deal
When it comes to you
Giving me updates
Of all the shit you do
So we don't bump into each other
As I'm passing through
Events, places, and things
That you might be at too
You see
They understand
I need my fix
So I don't lay hands on you
I even got to know your family
Cause you were stupid enough to put there info up there too
I've been to every family function you ever had
Even photo-shopped a pic of me shaking hands with your dad
I make memories out of air and frankly don't care
Because I fell in love
When we exposed our truths through cyberspace
Which I assumed meant that
Your heart was out for me to come chase
And then when you find out I'm as damaged as my page says
You try to leave
I should have warned you of the consequences before
I put my heart on my sleeve
However you are safe
As long as I pretend you didn't leave
And
As long as
I BELIEVE
You still love me
But soon I fear

My dependency on these lies
Will turn severe
And I'll start thinking
How no one else could have you
If you weren't here...

Random Thoughts of a Heartbroken Mind:

I realize your disconnect; now. As I replay our conversations
In my head I start to kick myself for not listening to me. The red flags
should have shot up when you spoke about friends but never
mentioned names. The alarms should have sounded when our
time was interrupted by your cell phone when before you
never took calls, text messages, or BBM's. Deep down I knew, but
didn't care. Because I thought, I would be the exception, the one to
stay. (Chuckle) What a fool I was.

I have survived love's many storms and fury. To be here. Without a
healthy concept of feeling or a whole heart. I'm not even sure what
pieces are left, every person discarding the pieces given to them. I
feel empty. I am throwing in the towel until this heart is healed or
the scars from my previous encounters are no longer visible to the
naked eye.

Your Thoughts:

_____
_____
_____
_____
_____
_____
_____
_____
_____
_____
_____
_____
_____
_____
_____
_____
_____
_____
_____

HEARTBREAKER

Random Thoughts of a Heartbreakers Mind:

I am not a heartbreaker by choice. I knew love once upon a time, we held each other through seasons and storms. She was the reason I woke up. The reason I listened to the radio comforted in the knowledge that every love song was about us. The nostalgic memories of our happiness, of us, are forever cemented in my mind. They taunt me now and send a bitter venomous poison through me that rots my core; with the fact that anything close to that love will never happen again. So, I will feast on your dreams, be a glutton for your love, and once satisfied. I will move on. Thanks for the snack.

In front of me, she took my heart and stomped on it. And with every step ground it deeper into the pavement, then spit on it for good measure. Then with angelic eyes she smiled, picked it up, and handed it to me saying "Here you go!". Shocked and stunned all I could say was "Naw you can keep that. Where I'm going, I won't need it". And ran away.

Some are born this way; to break hearts and change the course of people's lives through their lies and deception. But most, are made this way; once unafraid to love, they did and came head to head with cupids baby wrath of heartbreak, to become the heartbreaker, never to be vulnerable again.

Your Thoughts:

_____
_____
_____
_____
_____
_____
_____
_____
_____
_____
_____
_____

If I Can't Be With You

If I can't be with you
I'm breaking hella hearts, just to get through
So I can better handle your rejection
I'll make them cry
Uncontrollable tears that I cannot
And they will be my reflection
My pain.
Will be seen in their
 Broken Spirits;
And brittle hearts
This cycle
Will continue
Because I won't be happy
Unless it's with you
And if I can't be happy
Then fuck the world's happiness too
I will turn from
Nice guy to Asshole
Just to be with you
But if that doesn't work
Then sadly
This hole in my heart will stay
This lump in my throat won't ever go away
And no heart will be spared

Love Poem 137

You really don't want me to love you
I am love's fool
Don't let the sweet gestures fool you
I am crazy
And love uses me like her 2 dollar whore, bottom bitch
And I'm always happy to oblige my pimp
My lezzy love speed is like a corvette,
Going from 0-60 in 2.5
Its dangerous
With a price tag that's attached that requires
Your soul at the door
You really
Don't want me to be with you
Because I will love you hard.
Even if I don't mean it
Too desperate for love's
Affection to be truthful
Brutally honest
Mean even and tell you
You're not ready to be my inspiration
Not strong enough to serve as my muse
My soul not attached at all
So please don't speak of love
Cause I can fake it
While knowing
That
We won't make it
So, Your short term prey
Just some warmth to keep my urges at bay
So please don't speak of love
Cause we will never be ready for it anyway

Her Pain Is Our...

Her pain
Is our
Soundtrack
We dance
With lights off, music on
To her
Despair
Her cries
Are heard throughout the silent apartment
But
We...
Only see
Only feel
Each other
Keeping steady pace
Slow dancing
To her tears
At peace
Amongst this chaos
Her gasps for breath
In between sobs
Serves as our beat
And then...
We kiss
Dropping into the bridge
Ascending to worlds unknown
No longer in the cramped hood abode
We travel to a safe space
Surrounded by stars
This kiss
Came from the heavens
As
Her cries become uncontrollable
Expressing the built up frustration

Anger, sadness, pain
Disappointment

All let out at once
By a shriek
We smile
Continuing to kiss
Knowing her pain
All too well
Comfortable
In this moment
In tune with each other's presence
Acknowledging our pain
Never spoken
Holding tight to the embrace
Knowing that if we let go
We could fall from this paradise
Back to reality
Where we were never meant to be
Content in our fucked up ways
As
Possibilities become present ventures
Her agony
Strengthens our forever
Her cries equating
Karma's revenge times ten
But we don't care
Made hole again
 By this unfaithful union
Made closer
By her pain
That we caused
That plays in our mind
Forever as
Our
Symphony,
Soundtrack
Jingle of pain

We Almost....

We almost.....
Healed each other
Turning open wounds into distant scars and memories
Finding the shelter in each other's eyes
Making it possible to cry
To feel
To just be
100% Me, us
No matter what
We knew
Each other's thoughts were
Only of each other
I saw, your pain and allowed you to scream
Saw the not so visible scars of negligent parents
Who whored your soul out for a fix
Dismembering your insides
Stealing your identity
Causing you
To run the streets
Allowing adrenaline to be your fix
Chased by the nightmares through the day
So with
No peace
No trust
No home
And while trying to escape
The gutter that is your existence
You found
Another damaged soul
Beaten numb by sperm and egg donors
Not ready to be parents
And
In each other's arms
We allowed our outer masks down
Walls lowered
Moat drained
Guards gone

Panic room empty
And became reckless
Giving each other keys and passwords
To the towers we kept
Our true selves in
You allowed me to speak my power
And
I showed you how to smile
Yes we certainly did
Almost had everything
But I was afraid
Of being happy
Of explaining our union
Too stuck in other people's ways
I tricked you into a
Gasoline infused journey
To resurrection and bliss
Saw the dynamite
In your hand lit
And chose to abandon
This...
I could have saved you
But saved myself
For a change
No superman here
You found out
While confined to love's cage
Trapped their by my words
Of forever and chivalry
Your assisted suicide is long overdue
But at least I can
Admit
That.

Love's Traffic Ticket

I am speeding
past highways and byways
with precious cargo in the back
Hearts stolen from women who were stupid enough to give them to
me
I press on with no specific destination
Marshall Matthers LP keeping me company
Egging me on
The
5th of vodka gone
Shrooms consumed
Weed Smoked
Roaches eaten
Zoloft snorted
In failed attempt to
Change the scenery further
Numbing me for this ride
With these stolen hearts
Captured by
Lies told through fake smiles
Hiding my urge to dismember
I
Had
To get them
To teach them a lesson
The
Cop cars that chase
Want to arrest, and delay my journey
FUCK THEM.
I won't stop
Speeding
Towards the wall
It is beautiful
And
I know I cannot go through it

But
Can't go back to
High speed foot chases
With heart in hand
Given with trust and love
Trying to quickly reach paradise
Promised by fairytales and bullshit love stories
This wall is
Set up
To hinder progress
Permanently postponing happiness
Frustrating me to this point
I want to get used to the fire I have to look forward to
And I want these hearts to come with me
Going 120 mph
With Molotov cocktails in the back
I am ready for my close up
 Fuck you and your feelings and judgments
And
Fuck these hearts
That have been guarded and watch towered over
By those too scared to feel
The pain of the break
And the depression that
Comes with the actual physical ache
Because it is through my pain
That I truly live out my fate
And you will die and be reborn again
This time awake
WALL.
BOOM!!!

Pardon Me/Rant...

Pardon me,,, As I try not to grind my teeth in frustration, anger,
and despair after realizing after a short while that your fucking
boring and a complete waste of my time. And for staying after I came
to terms with this information.
But you had money.

Pardon me... For speaking the language most comfortable to me;
Distance, Silence, and Redirecting Energy and doing so because
I didn't want you to know anything about me. It was much more
interesting to try and fix your fucked up problems than talk about the
relationship you thought we were going to have.

Pardon me... For day dreaming while you're talking. It's through this
that I am able to escape to a better place so I can understand how I got
into
this present mess and how I'm going to leave to my future disaster.

Pardon me... For allowing the feeling of breaking your heart to
keep me happy, full of joy, goal orientated, & content
however leading you to believe that those feelings were caused by you.

Pardon me... For being immature; I used to be a nice guy. Until I saw all
Around me how this horrible way to be has bitches flocking to me. My
emotional immaturity puts a bulls eye on me seen by all the pretty
fishes in the sea. Besides you were bitter when I met you.

Pardon me... For not caring, for being just plain cold blooded, for
Being fucked up, and for doing what I want.
I mean,
I want love,
To be loved,
To show love.
Just not with you.

Pardon me for my imperfection and poor taste in sport....

But... Don't knock ANYTHING, till you try it.

Random Thoughts of a Heartbreaker's Mind:

Love has made a fool out of me too many times. For me not to understand that I won't be enjoying her gifts in this lifetime, so fuck it and everyone in it. Shit even the original versions of fairy tales were dark and twisted. Maybe that's the same story with love. It used to be known for its obscure tendencies and evil ways, which is why people had arranged marriages. Then somewhere the story got changed around, and love turned from evil to good, from darkness to light. And instead of a demon there was a little baby with arrows and rosy cheeks.

I cannot be vulnerable with you because I was vulnerable with her. I can lie to you because I told her nothing but the truth. I can cheat because I was faithful to her. I don't care about how you feel, because you aren't her. You are the runner up to an image of love's perfection that I know I can't be with.

Your Thoughts:

_____
_____
_____
_____
_____
_____
_____
_____
_____
_____
_____
_____
_____
_____
_____
_____
_____
_____
_____
_____
_____
_____
_____
_____
_____

Race Against the Sun

Fuck!!!
Once again I've
Come to
In a bed that is not my own
In a town that I don't live in
In nothing at all.
With a different female than my wife
I look out the window to see that it's still dark out.
And so starts my race against the sun.
Doing 90 on the highway
After the stale kiss and a hug from this person
That looks **NOTHING** like the woman I took home last night.
I press on.
Zoom!!!!!!
Past my morning breakfast options
I check the clock and its 5 in the morning
I got work in 3 hours
And I have left something over this Jane
Doe's house
Fuck it I'll get it later.
I can still feel the high from last night
Compliments of the weed
smoked, shots, and pills popped.
Desensitizing me
For the activities of the night before,
For today's excuse.
For this morning's goodbye,
And this shitty race against the sun.

Wash, Rinse, Repeat, Wash, Rinse, Repeat..
Conversation/Rant/Poem

OMG!!!!! I can't believe I did this shit AGAIN!!!!!!!!!!
Wash, Rinse, Repeat, (Hands) Wash, Rinse, Repeat (Hands)
Pound, Pound, Pound
O how my head
Echoes how the bed rocked last night
I'm shocked to realize it is 6am
should have been home hours ago
In bed
Hugging
Her, My wife
However,
Shower
WASH ass, Rinse, *Repeat?*
HELL YEA!!!!! YOU DON"T KNOW WHERE SHE'S BEEN!!!
Why the fuck do I keep doing this to myself?
I should of been broke up with this girl
Divorce the girl you call your wife?
HELL YEA!!!!!
THIS BITCH....
What?!?!
She got me a toothbrush and everything
Plottin Heifer Hoe
Brushing my teeth till they bleed.
FUCK!?!?!
Water, Rinse, Repeat, Rinse, Repeat
SWALLOW SOME BLOOD
I come out the bathroom
To look at what I thought was suppose to be a good fuck
But it was so bad I couldn't even fake a nut.
She looked like an AG
Walked like an AG
But fucked like a femme

PUNCH HER IN THE HEAD!!!!!!!
Naw, we gonna write a mean ass poem later
And Imma tell the homies she's

WACK!!!!!!!!!!!!!!!!!!!!!!!!!!
Still can't get a nut.
Start the race home
With a bullshit lie
That I got drunk
And passed out
Too tipsy to drive
And
She believed me
Making me realize the complete disconnect
If she knew me, she'd fathom the blatant disrespect
Can't believe she didn't catch that lie.
It was so fucking sketch I didn't even have a legit alibi.
If she had held it down
Hood rats wouldn't have ever come around
Infiltrating our home
Making me leave her alone
So now
She gotta deal
With lie filled
Pussy residue stained
Kisses
EEEEEEEEWWWWWWWWWW!!!!!!!!!!!
Go to the bathroom
Wash, Rinse, Repeat, Wash, Rinse, Repeat (Everything)

I Lie To You

I lie to you
To avoid this
Your eyes red from the dispensing of tears
Your screams and curses
My silence
Not knowing what to say
How to explain myself
Thinking my lies would spare you from this
They only prolonged the event
Of
Me seeing
You
In pain
Your disappointment in me
Your heart aching
Still you ask
WHY??
My lack of answers worsening the situation
Would rather be silent than tell you the truth
Would rather hold my tongue then allow it to unravel me
I understand that this truth
Will hurt you more
Causing your heart to not break but
Shatter
Into pieces
That can't be put together again
I lie to you
To avoid the conversation of
My fears and insecurities
Of you leaving

Of me completely falling
Of allowing you to have all of me
Of me, assuming this would not last
Don't want to explain how this is somewhat
Your fault
For not being there

For not holding me down
For not giving head like you used to
For leaving my ego un-stroked
For months at a time
But
My silence
Replaces my lies
As you try to understand..
But you can't fathom
The extent of my
Self sabotage
As I plan to fall
But keep females in my back pocket
Wanting to fully let go but
Needing a plan B
Like the morning after
A random fuck.
My lies I thought protected you
But they took away your options
To leave
To stay
To fight for me
Now I..
Am in a panic

Because one of my lies unraveled
Almost toppling the others
As news of my infidelity
Sends us to the clinic
Me
Not protecting myself
Now protecting myself
With this silence
Not sure what the news of the many others
Will cause you to do
To me
So my silence will save us
While Protecting the rest of my lies from unraveling
As I prepare myself

For the next time
Because you will take me back
Despite the results
And I will lie through my smile
Think of dead relatives to produce tears
Because the truth is
I don't want to be alone
And the real lie is
I want to be with you.

I Smell Like Her....

I smell like her thighs because you wouldn't allow me to taste you
Sick of a relationship with no desire, no lust, no passion
I'll take my chances out there.
I knew you, knew.
Just didn't care
The silence of your gaze as I walk in mirrors our relationship
Like a black hole it has sucked the light and the sound from us.
I remember when I told you, I loved you
My heart jumped as the lie left my lips
Causing pain in my chest that I did not show
My heart pissed cause I continue to say things in its name
However, you responded the same
Didn't know it was all gonna change
Didn't know that grown up words turned us into my parents
marriage
Devoid of love staying together for obligation
I have nothing because I left it all behind for you
For this....
This fucked up re-enactment of my childhood
I never wanted to lose myself for you.
I never wanted to race against the sun to come home to your face
Smelling like her
And tasting my lies
I was suppose to treat you like a queen
Who knew when the word love came around you would turn so
mean

Turning me into a zombie to the point where I had to dip off,
Had to leave.
But despite careful planning so I never see you
When I do
Your eyes are still as deep as I remember
Gripped with a pain
That can only be described with grunts, screams, and
convulsions
And I know I put some of it there.
You were my wife

Until you stopped my life
Got me leaving family and friends
In the end
I really did love you.
I just couldn't mean it and be with you.

Love Fades (a rant of sorts)

Our
Love faded like the memories of the conversations
We had in the
beginning
During that honeymoon phase
Before the flaws were introduced
Our disintegration
Started off slowly
With dreams I had for myself
Breaking off of me
Floating away
Fading into the distance of yester years
Replaced by US
And what WE could/would become
My,
Aspirations
Goals
I recalled
During afternoon smoke sessions
Where they
Recycled themselves back into my frontal lobe
And I began to
Recall what I was supposed to be
What I was
Before my dreams were deferred
By this, Us, A home, commitment
And I began to look elsewhere
To be emotionally, mentally, and spiritually vulnerable
To have my dreams nurtured
My thoughts
Listened to
Confusion set in only
When I reflected on happier times
When you actually listened
Instead of pushing me into a field
That best meets our financial obligations

We morphed into the superheroes
We thought
Each other needed
Abandoning the versions of ourselves
That brought us together
In the first place
Then...
Things snowballed
With small things
That were never corrected
Coming back to crush us
No more stolen kisses
or quickies
before leaving for work
No more cute messages
There was
No more stories
secrets
Or healing
The new happy memories
Became harder to grasp
Reserved for holidays, birthdays,
Dinner parties, and social gatherings
So when I, spoke of us
And smiled
I was working off the memory of us
With others
Realizing this
And feeling my guilt
I held onto those honeymoon happy memories of
Us
With a death vice grip
That blinded me from the real issue
Of our communication
becoming more and more scarce

As the secrets
Of new friendships
Locked us away in ourselves

We tried...
With half hearts to salvage this
Taking steps back
To recapture the paradise lost
Doing those things that
Brought us together in the first place
Before the recession
Before the financial troubles
Before our dreams changed
Forcing our paths further apart
Our attempts
To
Resurrect us
Didn't work
But we pretended they did.
And for a while
It seemed possible
To Fall in love with a stranger
Without mourning the person they used to be
But my emotional infidelity
Turned you into a familiar monster
And me
The distant lover
My stomach not being able to stand the sight of you
But my mind remembering that I used to be your lover
Yet not understanding how
We stayed together so long
Both refusing to speak our truth

That this love that was suppose to last past decades
Health issues
Famine
Family issues
Was no more
Instead our passive aggressive tendencies
Took turns for the worst
Both wishing the other would take the hint
As the
I love you's are said less to not at all

I'm too busy attempting to keep my image intact
To come home on time, or to notice
Using the same excuses, same lines
I,
Sought counsel
From friends who
Never liked you
And thus,
Encouraged an upgrade to this
Without specifying if I should do so still
In this,
So while finding comfort
In someone else's presence
We once
Passionate lovers
Turned into roommates
That occasionally
Fuck
Then
New friends became
Possible bed buddies

Occasional sex turned into no sex at all
and
By the time either of us acknowledged
the gap between us
Neither wanted to commit the energy
To building a bridge
Where there was once
Soil and foundation
Anger
Immediately follows the revelation
Weapons are drawn and
Poison dagger tipped phrases,
Secrets,
And low blows
Pollute the air
As Good friends pick up our pieces
As our love finally fades to

Black.

(But at least I'm finally free)

EGO

My ego
Stretches farther than the confines of your love can reach
Past the ways you make my heart stutter
And the butterflies in my stomachs flutter
Its
Filled with the dumbfounded sex faces of past lovers
Who didn't know I could do it like this
And we can't forget those
Sweet nothings whispered
In those first moments of bliss
The first impressions given
In those late night convo sessions.
That showed me as innocent
Even heaven sent
Opening them up to my spilling over can of worms
My true self brought to light by sticky situations of drama
Revealing my snake nature
Buried deep
As two battle over my one
Leaving me with only broken hearts to navigate as I slither away
Un-scaved
My ego
Fuels my fire
When my desire for this relationship is fading
Making me search for a hoe for hire
And since its materialism she aspires
Most likely she'll be basic reckless chick
To take your place when I'm done with
Your shit
To heighten the pain and bring insult with it
My ego
Doesn't care about your death threats
Tears cried
Hopes of this body laying by your side
All the way to the end
Because
You don't show it

Lucky for you,
You tell me every day
Cause other than that I wouldn't know it
My ego
Needs to know
How much you want me here
And it doesn't give a fuck about
How many people are there?
It wants you to fight for me
Show me passion
Put ownership through the way you touch me
Speak to me
Address me
Undress me
Walk with me
I say this because
My ego
Tends to bend reality
Making assumptions and seeing the proof
Sometimes makes an ass outta me
But
When the happy times are harder to grasp
Delayed and stopped by this world obstructing our path
It see's your hesitance
Acknowledges you're back and forth precedence
My ego then
Paints pictures of you leaving
Of your passion receding
It searches for the doubt in your eyes
The fear
That will cause you to abandon me
And it starts
With those awkward emotional relationships
In the hopes that you will fight to
Be the only one I confide in
My ego
Will purposely put you in awkward situations
In hopes to see what you do
With the sick need to see how you move

With the knowledge of me wanting her cake
But continuing to eat yours too
And if you don't regulate

Then this battle for my heart
You
Will lose.

I'm Sorry Poem

I...
Love you
So much it hurts
Past body, soul, mind, and spirit
You..
Are my constant
I would break skin with box cutter blade
To explain...
I miss you
I'm sorry
You are too good for me.
Please find someone else
Before my immaturity
Destroys what little faith you have in love
Leave me alone
My touch
You don't need
I can't handle it.
Your touch
Still foreign to me
This my fault
For not allowing You to explore the depths of my
Soul.
I gave you a key to a door
It just wasn't my heart
But I care for You like an old friend
Understanding that the love shared is deeper, stronger
Then physical bonds and binding
Can Illustrate
I would kill for You.
Which explains the attempts to destroy this flesh
I would kill anyone
Who treated You as I did.
My guilt
Eats at me

You.
Have to
Protect Yourself.
Which is why
I forced promises from Your lips
To protect You from me.
I love You
Enough to tell You
To run.
To see Your
Distance
And understand
Completely...
You want
To return
But
I know
You can't
You might love me enough to stay.
But I love You enough to
Push You away
You will hate me.
Your friends will despise me.
Just know.
I did this because
I
Love You.
Deep Breath
SHOVE...
Dedicated to:

_____

_____

_____

Random Thoughts of a Heartbreaker's Mind:

I sometimes feel bad for the good women destroyed in the crossfire's of my constant battle with the bullshit that is love and companionship. But at least I beat up their hearts instead of concentrating on their body, mind, and souls which were the much easier targets.

A true heartbreaker is never a lone for long. A true heartbreaker believes in the laws of karma but just doesn't care about the consequences. Everything changed after **that one:** got close, became familiar, than ran away.

Your Thoughts:

_____
_____
_____
_____
_____
_____
_____
_____
_____
_____
_____
_____
_____
_____
_____
_____
_____
_____
_____
_____
_____
_____
_____

SEXUALLY FRUSTRATED

I am horny. I am horny. I am horny. I am horny I am horny. I am horny. I am horny. I am horny I am horny. I am horny. I am horny. Need a nut. Need a nut. Need a nut. Need a nut. Need a nut. Need a nut. Need a nut. Need a nut. Need a nut. Need a nut. Need a nut.
I am horny. I am horny. I am horny. I am horny I am horny. I am horny. I am horny. I am horny. I am horny. I am horny. I am horny. Need a nut. Need a nut. Need a nut. Need a nut. Need a nut. Need a nut. Need a nut. Need a nut. Need a nut. Need a nut. Need a nut.
I am horny. I am horny. I am horny. I am horny I am horny. I am horny. I am horny. I am horny. I am horny. I am horny. I am horny. Need a nut. Need a nut. Need a nut. Need a nut. Need a nut. Need a nut. Need a nut. Need a nut. Need a nut. Need a nut. Need a nut.
I am horny. I am horny. I am horny. I am horny I am horny. I am horny. I am horny. I am horny. I am horny. I am horny. I am horny. Need a nut. Need a nut. Need a nut. Need a nut. Need a nut. Need a nut. Need a nut. Need a nut. Need a nut. Need a nut. Need a nut.
I am horny. I am horny. I am horny. I am horny I am horny. I am horny. I am horny. I am horny. I am horny. I am horny. I am horny. Need a nut. Need a nut. Need a nut. Need a nut. Need a nut. Need a nut. Need a nut. Need a nut. Need a nut. Need a nut. Need a nut.
I am horny. I am horny. I am horny. I am horny I am horny. I am horny. I am horny. I am horny. I am horny. I am horny. I am horny. Need a nut. Need a nut. Need a nut. Need a nut. Need a nut. Need a nut. Need a nut. Need a nut. Need a nut. Need a nut. Need a nut.
All love and no passion. PISSES MY PUSSY THE FUCK OFF!!!!!!!All love and no passion. PISSES MY PUSSY THE FUCK OFF!!!!!!!All love and no passion. PISSES MY PUSSY THE FUCK OFF!!!!!!! All love and no passion. PISSES MY PUSSY THE FUCK OFF!!!!!!!All love and no passion. PISSES MY PUSSY THE FUCK OFF!!!!!!!

And makes me want to cheat on you.

Random Thoughts of a Sexually Frustrated Mind:

I have relationships in which I can be emotionally, mentally, and spiritually vulnerable. THEY ARE WITH MY FUCKING FRIENDS!! The thing that sets you apart is that I want to have sex with you. But if your sex is wack, you might as well be my friend.

Anyone that says that sex is not an important part of the relationship is a stone cold fucking liar; and is most likely in a sexually stagnant and frustrating relationship right now.

It's not just about the sex. It's about vulnerability; it's about your willingness to give yourself to someone completely. Trust someone enough to touch you and heal the disconnect you feel between your body and your emotions.

Your Thoughts:

_____
_____
_____
_____
_____
_____
_____
_____
_____
_____
_____
_____
_____
_____
_____
_____
_____
_____

Send Me

Send me
Into another dimension
Send my heart dropping to my stomach
Send my back against the wall
Slammed hard against the cold
Clothes ripped
Send me signals with your eyes
When I walk in the door
Letting me know
That I will not be getting any work done tonight
Send me into ecstasy as screams and moans go
Throughout our home
Send me into...
A vortex filled with passion, lust, intensity
Send me into a spasm making my pussy spit
While you fuck, suck, and lick every part of me
Send me something beyond flowers, candy, roses and soft kisses
Send me fire in your eyes
Send me to work smiling and singing
Send me floating on a cloud out the door
And feed me strawberries
While I'm recovering from what you did to me
On the bedroom, bathroom, and kitchen floor
Send me out with scratches
And bite marks where others can see
Send me anything but chivalry
Send me anything but politeness
Send me your tongue down my throat
Send me raw and uncut
Triple X Fuckin
Because anything else you send to me will not pass
Make it known that you want me
And remind me...

And everyone else
Whose pussy this is.

TOUCH ME

Baby I need you to
Touch me...
It's strange...
That this is embarrassing to ask
From a lover
Who should know
My needs
But Seriously..
I need you to
Touch me in a way I am not used to.
Do something different
Take me out of my zone
Reach inside me and surprise me
With the new ways you touch, lick, tease, and please me.
Restrain my arms so I am unable to restrain myself
From the pleasure that you are about to give me.
Nibble, bite, and tease me.
Baby Please.
I need something more.
I'm allowing you to re-explore
Me
Do all the things you wanted to do
But never told me
Anything to get out this boring routine
Where you get between
My legs
And do what you do
Make out with me for a little
And then we're through
Because
It is at this point
That I realize that I was never truly touched by someone
Never taken to those places
Where my body just can't handle it anymore
And I would like to go there with you
I need blind passion

A lack of restraint
Domination
Because I don't want you or I to leave,
I don't want this dream to end.
And I don't want to ever think
About us
Ever being
Just friends.

My Fantasy...

I am not a picky person and therefore will be easy to please
I want to be overpowered, dominated, fucked by someone.
I want to be undressed with your eyes
And raped by your gaze
Look at me like you want me and take me
I want aggression
Fuck ME GODDAMN IT!!!!
Be diligent in your mission to make me remember
Your name
Fuck me like you mean it
Touch me all over.
Tell me how you feel with a stare, a glance, make your actions
Scream over your words.
In plain English
I want you inside me.
Make me wet with your presence
Show me how aggressive you can be
Talk dirty to me
Make me your whore
Take my spots and
Use them to your advantage
Drive me crazy
Lust for me
Just fuck me right.
Please.
Make me feel good
Make me feel good
Make me feel something.
So my appetite can come back.

Actions Over Words/Sexually Frustrated...A Rant of Sorts:

I DO NOT want your words. Tell me you want me without the use of
your pick-up lines, naughty conversation, compliments and Eskimo
kisses.
Touch me as if it were your last time.
Show me as I show you. Because I will not
remember every wonderful thing you say to me, but I will
NEVER forget how you showed me you loved me. How your body voiced
your passion. The very sound of it sending a ringing,
tingling sensations throughout me that vibrates and pulsates when
it reaches my clit. Watch me with
sinful intent, do something to show me that
these feelings that I have are mutual. Your words cannot
be my foundation. Because they will fail, lines cross,
and turn sour. Give me something I can stand on. I need the knowledge
and
facts that can only come from your actions. Notice me, look at me or just
act like you want me here.
....
I don't know what else to do, that would convey my needs any
better. We have had all the talks I can handle. Where I slightly
embarrass myself by telling you I need more from you
sexually, only for my words to be met with blank stares and
confusion. As you listen yet tell me in your nicest way possible that
you are unwilling to compromise. But, you knew... Prior to us
getting into this that I needed at least three nuts a week for me to
function properly and my eyes not wander. I have given you
intimate massages when you got home from work, surprised you
with rose petals, hot tub, and a dinner for us, complete with the
body chocolate and you can't even give me head with a ting of
enthusiasm; can't even walk me on the leash that YOU bought for
me. This is not going to work. And despite the comfort I have in
this relationship I have to venture elsewhere so that I can continue
to do this housewife thang for you. Sorry... I guess. But I have
given you too many chances, written too many poems, given you
too many motherfucking hints for you to be at all surprised with
what I have to do now.

Mind Fuck

With her tongue
She stripped me of my mask
Leaving me baron and naked
Fully exposed
With nowhere for me to hide
She
saw me vulnerable
Tripping and stuttering over my words
Attempting to cloth myself
Her words hit my skin
Penetrating the layers and barriers to my soul
Giving me goose bumps
As they
Healed wounds
Leaving no scars
Teasing me
With her private introduction
To the English language
Setting the pace
Her hands everywhere
With her graceful tongue
Writing chapters of my life
That are peaceful
Her whispers
Warm my hole
As she traces
Haiku's of loving words
On my nipples
Keeping me present
And
Bone, tissue, and muscle
close
Her verbs
Supporting her actions
To give me pleasure
Her tongue gave me
A dissertation on how I

Make her feel
By the time I actually
Had something to say
Besides
O Shit
I was
CUMMING!!!
I came to and
She was gone
And I was
Sprawled out on my bedroom floor
What a MIND FUCK

I Will Not Touch...

I will not touch myself tonight...
For too long I have accepted
Orgasms from my own hands
While my lover sits idly by and does nothing
Not anymore.
My body refuses it
I am
Longing for the touch of another
Longing for a touch unfamiliar
Longing for a touch of passion
Longing for a nut
Not by my own hands
Not anymore
My body aches for a touch
My fire builds
My headaches worsen
Words get snappy
body tenses up
Waiting for a release
Waiting to get someone's FULL UNDEVIDED ATTENTION
Waiting, waiting, for the touch of another to satisfy this need
To be wanted
What I really need
Is to finally, completely
CUM
In a violent shake that sends me to
Paradise anywhere
And makes me forget my name
And scream yours.

Your Secret.

As I sit here
In this pill and weed
High
My mind starts to drift
To
Late Night
Rendezvous
Of our first encounter
I smile
As I imagine how it is to kiss you
Not as a friend
Just as...
See,
I don't know
The words to describe an, us
Are unheard of
Not to be spoken of to anyone
But I have...
Caught wind that you know
How my eyes wander about your body
I try to catch your gaze
Then shyly avoid it
My eyes...
Give me away
I often stare too long
Getting caught
Drifting off into a daydream
Where we're fucking
But
You apparently know
The secret that eats me
And Yet ...
Say nothing
Do nothing
You watch me struggle
With this silent rejection that kills
Me..

Once
I caught you staring at me
So boldly and
I thought
That you might
Be open
To.
Take a risk
Even if the risk is our
Friendship
To show how we feel
About each other
With no barriers
Let me ease that
Loneliness
That I see hiding in your eyes
You cover it up with
Smiles but I see
The stress that eats at you
And I am
Begging you for
A chance to give you
 relief
Amongst this chaos
I wish...
I could do more
Wisk you away
To foreign lands and secret hiding places
And make sure you never worry
Want or need anything
But for now....
I give you support
Through my friendship
But please listen to my plea;
I can keep this secret
Just like your others
Please, friend
Let me
In.

Touching Her/ Thinking Of You

She....
Was a past lover
Separated
By a fork in the road on my journey
We met again
Feeling lonely
Topped off the night with
Vices
Allowing us to flow, feel, experience, freely
Without guilt
I.
Jump in.
Start to touch.
And then.
Your face pops up
Fucking up my concentration
luckily my hands are on auto-pilot
remembering the curl of her lips
they continue...
Understanding that she isn't wet enough
Play with her more
She smiles at their memory
However,
I am still thinking of you
Your ass fatter
Breasts bigger

You sound better speaking Spanish than she does
Would rather listen to you moan than her
Your skin smoother
Your pussy wetter
My hands love being inside you
Fuck...
I'm still inside her
Thinking of you
Eyes Open

Your face bleeds into hers
Thank God the lights are off
I close my eyes and think of you
She is moaning loudly
I am angry now
SHUT THE FUCK UP!!!!!
I want to scream
Cause she doesn't sound like you.
My part is over.
My heart nor head in it.
I lay back
Preparing to sleep this off
OMG!!!!!
She is trying to give me head
Your face is flashing across my eyes
Your naked body being my motivation
But her tongue doesn't feel like yours
I can't cum
Despite my forced efforts
I bring her up with a kiss
Rolling over to sleep
Feeling guilty
Because I knew before

That yours was the only touch
I wanted
and needed
However, you refuse my touch
Worried that feelings will follow
So now I must walk this
World.
Touch less
And alone.
FML.

Random Thoughts of a Sexually Frustrated Mind:

You didn't learn my body because I didn't trust you to do so, you couldn't touch me because I knew you couldn't take me to the heights I needed to reach and you never showed me the passion I desired. These are the reasons why my eyes wandered so frequently when walking down the street. They are the reasons why I always kept those numbers given. They are the reasons why I began to shut down emotionally and the reasons why we aren't together now

I have been frantically searching for the sex that matches or tops the one that broke my heart. Because despite the fact that she was an asshole. When she put her hands on me, I had no doubt whatsoever that I was her lady, that she wanted me, and I was safe in letting her have me (even if I really wasn't).

After exhausting my little black book and calling the last of my ex's, there is no one left. No more friends, of friends to be set up with. I guess I have to take my chances out there, on the outskirts of my sterile lezzy bubble. Guess I have to start making new friends again. UGH FUCK!! >:O

Your Thoughts:

_____
_____
_____
_____
_____
_____
_____
_____
_____
_____
_____
_____
_____
_____
_____
_____

Please Don't.....

Please don't
Be touching me
And playin games right now
I understand that you want to tease me
But my pussy's already wet
Please don't stall
Because I have shit to do and
I barely know you
And have no time for some temporary
Bullshit romance
Please don't
Ask questions
Not after you talked yourself up
So high we fuckin in the bathroom
Please don't bite me
Cause that's just fucking rude
BITCH
I want no marks of remembrance of this fling
Please don't...
Ask to exchange numbers
I'm **NOT** going to call you
Please don't
Talk
Because your words mean nothing
Please don't
Be surprised by my coldness
I've separated
My body from emotions
PLEASE DON'T.....
Talk like that.
Saying stupid movie and pick up lines
Designed to make me feel special
Unless you want love to replace like in
All my sentences and poems about you
You cannot handle my intensity
And I will not be making any investments
Guaranteed to crash and burn

So.
PLEASE DON'T
Look at me like that
Eyes searching my soul for answers
I refuse to get trapped in your gaze
Because I have seen what they have to say
So don't lie about love that lasts past decades
When your eyes tell a different story

The Way You....

The way you
Touch me
Sends my pussy into a furious rage
Which causes my hands to ball up into fists
So that I might teach you a lesson
Screaming racial and ethnic slurs
Questioning your gayness
While I attempt to rip strands of your hair out with one hand
And black your eyes with the other
The way you.
Touch me
Is incorrect
You have failed this test
Doing my pussy no justice
Causing frustration to take the place of my excitement
The way you
Look at me
Lets me know that you
Believe
You've
Held it down
Put in work
Broke my back
Got me bout to clean house and make breakfast
You STUPID BITCH JERK!?!?
Your False.
Your lucky I'm broke
Cause I would trash your house
And beat you
Your disrespect being the cause
All this and

Your eyes burn with
Intentions of
Making me re-live this horror
Of your hands

Doing nothing
Irritating my pussy
Causing my fire to leave
And me wishing I would have just
Sucked it up
And masturbated to
Short preview sessions
On dirty websites
Instead of being...
With you
The way you....
Lick me
Makes my pussy believe there's an epidemic going on
Of bad head
And causes me to
really think you have an attraction to the penis
The way you..
Handle this pussy
Makes me see red
As I become the embodiment of my pussy's frustration
I wanna kick you in the clit
The way you...
Look
Fooled me
I took into account
your hand size
Your broad shoulders
Stocky arms
With assumptions that
Your hands would be able to reach deeper

Hitting my G-Spot causing
Changed sheets in the morning
Me not caring the I had to sleep in the wet spot
Your broad shoulders able to handle my scratches and bites
Creating stability as we move
Rock, Shake,
The foundations of this bed
Of my world

And this house
And your solid body would control the pace, tempo, beat, and be strong enough
To go the distance of this journey.
Making sure that neighbors know your name
But...
I was wrong...
Fooled by
The way you...
Speak
Which painted a picture
Of
You laying my ass out
Of me
Meeting my sexual match
Being able to finally let go
Finally be touched by someone who doesn't need lessons
Because they pay attention to the sounds my pussy makes
And they know which way to go
The way you...
Touch me does nothing but
Produces hatred in my eyes
Causing blood to boil
I want to put your face through a wall
Because the way you touch me
Taste me
Explore me
Was not what I wanted

Or what my pussy needed
At all.
So Fuck you...
You
Bad pussy eatin
Pillow Queen
Fucking lying poo-put bitch!!!!

Sex Slave

This bed is my prison
Your arms are my shackles
You're eyes torture me
Burning with passion
Enough to fuel us both
As I find myself back at your feet
As you asked.
Needing to touch
To feel remembered
To feel important
To be validated
So when you want me
To touch, kiss, and lick your body
I will come
And do my job.
Forever sentenced
To this cell
Of desire
The need to be close
To someone
As your body screams and begs for me
Mine doesn't
But I haven't yet learned to say no to such a request
Prepared to do whatever
To stay true to my name
This is for my twisted honor
And I always do my best
To please
Living up to my low expectations
My indifference towards you
You don't seem to notice
Since
I still kiss.
I still touch.
Understanding that this is all you want
All I need

What I am here to do
You
Batting your eyes,
Talking and such
Does nothing
But prolong the main event
I gaze through you
To possibly qualified applicants
You mistake this for passion
As you unknowingly watch me try to feel something
That coincides with what I am about to do
I flashback to the
Conversations that led to flirting
As I purposely steered
You into
This exotic exchange
Hounded by the urge to touch something
To try to feel something
To replace this emptiness
With your cum
Your screams
As the only sounds I make
voice the
Strain of my work
This is my curse.
Violently looking
Frantically searching
For the passion filled kisses
That can only come from new flesh
Another notch on my belt

You can't save me
And don't want to
If you did,
I would never have ended
Up in your bed so quickly
Tasting your waters
Feeding off your energy
Draining your life force

So just shut the fuck up
Stop talking,
And enjoy the ride.

Love's Eternally Twisted Lessons:
(The Rules of Never with a Caution, Poem thang)

NEVER compromise
NEVER stay if you don't want to.
If this book has touched you in anyway, then you've felt it, the
promise of a new beginning, a better you all wrapped up in another
person; their light shining so bright that it allows you to grow into a
stronger, wiser you. However, even in the midst of love, with it
tangible deep down you know that it is
far too easy to fall from love's grace. And with all the baggage this
human life brings you have to be able to admit that even if you
give your "all", love another human unconditionally, that, that might not
be enough, to save them or keep them from turning back into the
strangers they once were.

SO

NEVER compromise your foundations
NEVER change the core of who you are for another.

WORDS OF CAUTION
If you chose to love so dangerously, giving the pink slip to your
Body, being, and your heart; become dependent on that
person for your sun. You need to accept that nothing lasts forever,
not even your compatibility, not even your love. And **YOU** alone
have to be strong enough to pick up the pieces of yourself and put
them back together again(when and if your love fades to black).
You have to be whole either way, because only a whole person
can survive heartbreak, without longing for what once was,
searching for it's replica everywhere, or turning into a hurt
bitter person that goes around hurting other people.

AND

If you're honest enough to admit that, you're not quite there yet.
It's okay. Just love yourself for a while and let love come find you.

NEVER lose your voice, always say what you need to say.

Live, Love and experience life boldly and freely without shame. You're a human fucking being, I suggest you enjoy the experience.
Don't let the fear of pain/failure/heartbreak stop you from experiencing and feeling everything (or as much as you can safely handle). Don't let past mistakes make you timid and standoffish towards life and living yours to the fullest. Every day is a new day to change your stars and love yourself more. Besides, it is when your living your life to the fullest that you will meet the person(s) that will stay with you while Karma's fucked up revenge is inducing lesson learning change agents of havoc into your life that will cause you to grow and deal with/face your shit (the trick is though, that you can't be looking for them or love either ☺ Ha-ha, Damn you cupid).

So

Jump into the abyss of yourself
Into a pool of your reflection
Tread the waters of your past
Break free
From the skeletons
That stalk you
Polluting your soul with their mal intent
Forgive yourself
And survive being swallowed
By your whale of regret
Burst out as the whale
Exhales
Into your brilliance
And float
On the life raft of your
Hopes, dreams, and childhood aspirations
And once your there
You will touch the shores
of your soul
To bring balance to the yin and yang
that encompasses you

There you will battle
Your desires, jealousy, lust
fears, darkness
Hidden secrets and desires
So after you've
Delivered a bear hug blow
To your shame
Accompanied with the kiss
Of death's humble understanding
You will lay on the beach of your forever
Baking in your inner light
At peace with you
And those decisions
Of yester years
That made you,
You.
And once there
Right there
You will find another
On the same journey of understanding
A similar epic quest
To a more honest version of themselves
And
Together
You will dive into yourselves
And
Find
In each other
Your reflections
So...
Choose Wisely
Choose Yourself
And wait
For the Random
Blip in time
When love
Chooses
You..

Good Luck ☺

www.ingramcontent.com/pod-product-compliance
Lightning Source LLC
Chambersburg PA
CBHW031522270326
41930CB00006B/484